MW01625495

A ROOM IN THE HOUSE OF TIME

POEMS

Kip Zegers

2020

DOS MADRES PRESS INC.
P.O. Box 294, Loveland, Ohio 45140
www.dosmadres.com editor@dosmadres.com

Dos Madres is dedicated to the belief that the small press is essential to the vitality of contemporary literature as a carrier of the new voice, as well as the older, sometimes forgotten voices of the past. And in an ever more virtual world, to the creation of fine books pleasing to the eye and hand.

Dos Madres is named in honor of Vera Murphy and Libbie Hughes, the "Dos Madres" whose contributions have made this press possible.

Dos Madres Press, Inc. is an Ohio Not For Profit Corporation and a 501 (c) (3) qualified public charity. Contributions are tax deductible.

Executive Editor: Robert J. Murphy

Illustration & Book Design: Elizabeth H. Murphy
www.illusionstudios.net

Typeset in Adobe Garamond Pro
ISBN 978-1-953252-02-9
Library of Congress Control Number: 2020944019

First Edition

Published by Dos Madres Press, Inc.

ACKNOWLEDGEMENTS

Some of these poems have appeared, or are about to appear in *Barrow Street, Broad Street, Hanging Loose, North Dakota Quarterly, The Literary Review, Urban Arts,* and *The Wisconsin Review.*

Dedication: This book is for Jill, who listened to most of these poems when they were new and annoying. And for Christopher Chilton and John Loonam, the after school group, who helped these poems grow.

Photo of the author: Jill Crandall

TABLE OF CONTENTS

I.

II.

III.

I.

The Turn

—after Vallejo's "Pilgrimage"

The dead who make no shadows on the road,
who speak beneath silences and make no sound,
walk with me. We go along together,

the mild father with his banjo his camera his exile,
the taut mother with her books her Marlboros
and a puzzle she never finished,
the favorite aunt gone deaf and blind
who hides a photo of herself as lovely girl
in the pocket of the last housedress she put on,

they are civilians after battle
trailing an army headed somewhere,
or guides with booklets they cannot hand out
as they walk, and walk,

these whose endurance is not muscular,
who do not expect to be heard as they
call out but make no sound:
a silence I begin to understand.

Another Thing My Father Did

-1-

In the father's story, war whispered
"you own nothing but these tin, neck-worn tags."
From Okinawa, he placed his lost
address like a prayer in daily letters
home. His son found them after the end.

When the father came home from the war
and his son was almost 3, the father
would have held back, waiting, to see.
When the father came home from the war
his son was confused – who? – three
in the house? Once, when they wrestled,
the boy struck out, the father doubled over,
the son closed his eyes.

-2-

In the son's story war is a silent man
reading, peering out at *Victory at Sea*
on the new TV, score by Richard Rogers,
destroyers plow the South Pacific, and
each week, Navy wins.

The father who'd come home from the war
took them to swim. At Touhy Avenue beach,
the lake lay flat, empty of swimmers, icy under
a burning sky. The father said, "Prairie winds
send our lake's warm water all the way
to Michigan." The boy, at four, would not
try a toe. Timid son. Long after, the son holds
a photo he's found: the father, still gaunt, pale,
has his arm around his son;
they are keeping an eye on that lake.

Lines Composed on the 1 Train

- after Robert Pinsky

On the train and walking around inside
a poem of one man's mother
I heard, "that's what I get for showing off,"
my mother's voice, gasping as she reaches
to shelve a can, she grunts,
then, as if felled by a blow
sinks to the linoleum, the body
limp, the eyes lost, I remembered
that I'd just flown in,
she had asked me to shop, I had shopped,
and house bound, chair bound, she'd risen
to be normal, to help, and a can
slipped, collapsed she spoke
her last words – then

a woman on the 1 train was shouting
"…*I am* the boss of this. That school is nothing
to us. They are strangers that you see each day.
We take nothing that they have. *You* tell them *that*."
"…I can't!" cried the boy. The mother lowered
her voice, the boy's eyes did not leave her face
as she spoke, 168 St. was announced, riders
stared ahead or at devices in their hands, I saw
my mother back from the kitchen phone
to dinner, the waiting table, her guests,
"Gordon's gone," she whispered, and sat,
and ate, looking at no one,
her baby brother the pastor, estranged

since she'd married a Catholic, was dead.
She was the boss of a silence in which
her guests ate what sat before them,
she was the boss of not being where her body was.
Guests left quickly.

I wanted my father to hold her, weeping,
but broken she was splinted with silence
keeping bones aligned that did not heal.
What I'd been reading on the train was Pinsky,
poem with a mother whose silences
and departures were a knot
soaked in cold water. That mother,
an enigma, rose inside a poem,
walked out the other side,
but never left. Sons cannot look away.

I see my mother trying,
tripped up, totaled, "this
is what I get for showing off."
I see again eyes emptied,
the mouth gone slack, death
as the boss of silence. Now
her bladder empties on the kitchen floor,
and such is death, unable to see
me standing, unable to turn away.

Backyard

At 89 my mother said, "I am not afraid."
She was shrunken, alert, it was her real voice.
They say my grandfather stood in Wilson Avenue,
raising his cane, stopping cars so he could cross
to visit Coleman, the undertaker.
Grandpa's long gone; Coleman, not so fast.

"Aunt Mae can see us from where she is,"
said one of the nuns from a chair in Coleman's Parlor.
I thought she must have had a line of sight
that passed through shingles and plaster. And yet
Aunt Mae had whispered at the last, "Take me
home sweet Jesus," and so left Ravenswood Hospital

once for all. I stood beneath the apple tree,
having been asked to take down what I'd ridden
in childhood, my own crow's nest, that triple fork
now decayed. The big branch leaned, whine
of chain-saw, my father pulling to stop "that damn
tree" from scraping his house, held a rope,

the tree cracked, slapping him with its thick
green hand. Covered to the waist with apple leaves,
flat on his back on the lawn he'd never been happy with,
stunned, sheepish, beginning to be fine,
"That's enough for today," he said, "enough
is enough." But it never is. The body of the

mother on her bed could still be spoken to.
Whatever she heard. Her worn shirt rose and fell
beneath the D.N.R. she'd taped to the wallpaper.
The dead body of the mother was
out of reach. When I spoke to it
mine was the voice from here on out.

Another Letter to Whitman

I'm not the first, Walt, it's complicated.
I've worn my father's dog-tags, then
gone out, his metal on my flesh.
His heart when he wore them, his secrets

were his own, but men need fathers.
When his father died, my father showed
no emotion. I stood beside him in church
waiting for it, and what death meant.

Walt, you wrote this about your father: "strong,
self-sufficient, manly, mean, angered, unjust,
the blow, the quick loud word, the tight bargain,
the crafty lure..." He died with your words in print;

had you maybe reconciled, or just stood there,
for years? I did not call my father names,
I was ashamed of him, at 16. An ulcer, sign
of a boy high-strung and soft, was what I had.

Heartburn, indigestion, vague complaint
was the flag I rode under in my 20's. Just
own your stomach, Olivia said; own yourself.
I thought she was kidding. What my father had

was *swallowing*. He'd rise from dinner, go stand
at the window hiccupping, spitting up into Kleenex.
My mother turned away. I watched, ashamed.
Then he and I grew old, one at a time.

Now I imagine my dad watching, standing
outside of time, where he can see me pass.
As he sees I see him, he winks. It lights his face.
I had to birth him, here, to see that happen.

Family Math

i.

the last time I saw her
she came up behind me on
the couch, she rested her hand on
my neck I flinched away a thing
I'd done before – bad timing.

"Let's have ham tonight!" She was
cheerful I was there, finally, even
always flinching. Perhaps
she thought it was all she deserved.
I thought she seemed better, this visit,
then when I came back with the meal,
unpacking it – she collapsed

– I placed the emptied body on her bed.

"I loved you too much," I heard,
myself say, surprised to hear
spilled words. And after,
with phone calls to make,
details to settle, I had that sentence
like a dial tone in the hand when a call
connected breaks.

ii

back when my dad was dying,
I, visitor, found their door open,
her bed empty, peeked in, saw
there in his narrow bed the two of them,
she holding him, he exhausted, being held,
her pleased face, two who had

in my seeing never once held hands,
or hugged, or sat close together
on the couch were now a gate,
its two halves latched. I said something
dumb like, "Hi," or "I'll just go
get the paper." She was holding what
she was losing, proud to be seen?

iii.

When I saw her seven years later
she came up behind me I was facing away
on the couch, she rested her hand
on the back of my neck I flinched away.

Truth here is sorrow stripped of varnish,
bare wood facts which, really, are not new.
I recall the woman and the man,
lives that held disaster, steady work,
many books, some good luck, and the one child.
I see a man, a few years older than I am now,
low in his illness, an old woman
with clogged arteries, each exhausted,

if they could speak to each other, he'd wonder,
"Is he finished with us, at last?" She'd answer,
"Still so wordy, such a talker!"
And now I see them sleeping, at rest.

II.

What Must Be True

It was teacher's pride, telling a mother
of her daughter's brilliant essay,
the uncle who swam away from China, "but
my brother drowned," the mother said
with a shake of the head,
"he did not make it," – there was a minute left
on parent/teacher night –
"she does not want to remember
a story must be true."

Truth is in things I remember I have
not stopped remembering. In mid-March
this might mean inch high points of leaf,
like bright green fingernails in the mud,
will claw up from under to be daffodils.
I have a daughter. Right now
she'd be on a train, Brooklyn
to "the city." I cannot imagine
her thoughts there with other women
and the lost, the staring, the angry, the late
to school. Her work-street is cement
barriers, cold-eyed police
deployed by recent events, and now
she might be walking that street
once the wall of a Dutch city. Theirs
would also not have been gentle times.

What “true” might also mean is what my own
mother said, and she rarely spoke,
“I’m not afraid.” She looked up, held, then looked away,
a visitor, I’d been trying to ask
what she needed not to talk about.
I also remember being fond of the girl
whose mother insisted on story-truth,
a delicate, sensitive girl, then,
we learned, don’t get in her way.

Today, in pre-dawn dark, I stood out
with newspaper, trucks roared in the valley,
first robins singing, I saw by streetlight,
tulips two inches high
also do not know how to stop.

A Thing Made Of Other Things

"I think there is no hope for us
but in meaning." -George Oppen

Late night Stop 'n Shop, sticky littered tar,
who-gives-a-shit-in-this-heat-shoppers,
carts half full, heads down marching silent
stupefied irritated sweat. Such silence
undoes us in the city's blinded swirl.
Next, in daylight, "You're the felicitator...",
that's Charlie being cute, in a room downtown,
10 writers becoming pages of what rises
when silence anchors and abides, like hope.

And after, on sweating Delancey Street,
a waitress: "you got to grind the sesame
... like this ... add to sauce, dip noodles
then. How *could* you know if none before *me*
told you?" Her smile, mischievous,
made words real. And sweetly cold
the noodles. Cash only. Then the play
we'd come for. A single human voice
fills the full up space we've entered.
I sat reassured by the world and its pain
in the hands of a man who works inside them
laughing and enraged. We went raw outside:

I remember steaming streets still teeming
with traffic on tires and high heels I remember
the silent steady smiling cabbie mastering
massed streets I remember our train
made empty by a man explaining baseball

to a wife whose face was turned away I thought
words can empty a space I remember
station stop Spuyten Duyvil and blackness
under sky high Henry Hudson Bridge I remember
few cars waiting, and how one there lit up,
I remember the dark behind us silent,
the way rich black dirt is quiet growing grass.

The Ride In

"Our faith comes in moments;
our vice is habitual." -Emerson

Down from the Bronx to clotted Dyckman,
then south reading Emerson on "The Poet"
to Park Avenue, under the grim tracks,
east on 132 into Harlem rebuilt or refaced:
Envy Nails, Grab 'n Grow Grocers, Retail Space
Available, white people walking, owners now,
one guy waving *Wall Street Journal* flags a cab,
a man to trip over, and not fall –

I blink and July, '67, is outside on 5th
at 129th: the broil, traffic overheating,
news of Newark riots rising from radios
as I, a young man, leaving work, watched
wipers sweep hydrant spray, kids at play
taunting traffic, fear's big eyes behind glass,
drivers trapped. The sky sagged low and yellow,
the avenue a tunnel as bodies of buildings
leaned in, foreheads seeming to touch.
On one corner men with chains and chunks
of lumber. The other side, 10 cops in a van.

It was chance not miracle things did not get worse.
And in a room around the corner dining
on franks 'n beans, I remember thinking,
"Langston Hughes once lived a block away,"
a fact, solid in uncertain air. Another is

in war a hole in earth burst open,

three men down, one, George Oppen,
gone teacher and poet, was blooded, but
between him and shrapnel were two others;
by chance, he lived. And buried his dog-tags, H
for Hebrew, at the fox-hole he crawled up from
but never left: a place can not explain itself,

upper 5th Avenue, at 116th Street now.
A student never forgotten lived near here.
With her grandmother was all each had
in the world. Years after, on the street, she
was hurried, no time to see if Now, for her,
was enough. Next is Central Park, shining as if

the doormen of all great buildings had
polished it for others to use. I'm walking now
on 98th as, reading, a little girl emerges
from a gleaming door, and reading,
passes beneath a canopy, and reading,
enters a black car. It's her ride to school.

I rode with Mr. Emerson father of poets
who said, *You* can. *You* have already arrived
at the place. He might have meant the ride in,
the swirl widening within it, like an eddy in time.
Once I saw, from a bridge on Bronx River,
a circling in the current, a leaf drawn in,
a scrap of paper spun away, an eddy peopled
with pieces from places upstream.

Dependable

I have, and have had often, a dream
of time travelling to see Walt Whitman
at Fulton Ferry, 1855. If, arrived,
I somehow held a photo from a book
to be printed in 1970, and looking up

I picked from many one man's hopeful eyes;
one man simmering from many uneasy;
one young at 37 from others immature;
or from the root-bound, one man slow to grow,
– Whitman at the ferry – then I would wave,
but it's two in the morning right here,
and my thoughts, without defenses on,
are now of Walt who left us words
like stepping stones in the sucking mud,

he's our still-standing ancestor, a specter
in the fouled emergency room of now,
holding back madness with original verse,
if that is not asking too much
of verse

Next

From where he sat on the floor before
and between classes, he never looked up,
his stillness never opened its steel door.
What, between his face and shoes, did he see?

The local homeless man, a kind of neighbor,
sleeps in the park on a board set on crates.
I saw him at dawn, hour at which many
dogs are being walked. Dogs will spend the day

waiting for what's next, life to resume.
The boy waiting behind his slack legs,
cornered by his refusals, only nodded
his emptied face; my neighbor *did* speak,

"they're trying to poison me," "that damn thief."
It was bottles and cans. Today, pink afghan,
black hoodie, asleep inside public court #2,
tennis players rousting him will be

what's next, and the boy, a senior, beaten
long before he could begin, asked if he was up
for a job come fall, said, "No. If I got hungry
it might have nothing there for me to eat."

Up

First, the girl who wrote how, mid-test,
the numbers on her paper came loose
then fled, spilling off the page to
flow across her desk and fall
to floor, a swarm of scurry,
lines of black ants getting random,
as she panicked the guy beside her said,
"I can see from where I sit how much you need
a Math Catcher," then he reached into air
and pulled from there a cardboard box
whose feet were feelers feeling for numbers
right away. This would he said
do the trick, it was quite a trick
she was wielding when
her teacher, rudely, called, "Time!"
took her emptied page by one of its corners
with two fingers, "Emily. You seemed
more than a little distracted today."

Then the boy who wrote of nights in a bucket
his parents lowered, dripping and mossy,
into the circular, parents who smiled
with their teeth and cursed each other,
never him, bucket-bound, the boy
whose days in school were floating
up a thread to watch kids busy
being good, while he, spider like, upside
and ceiling high, broom free, had his web,
and wove weirdness with it.

I have not, years after, forgotten these
of those who stood inside the difficult
and spoke. This is my version
of their versions. Names and what year
are lost, still these are of alchemy,
and they alchemists for real,
making precious from the raw.

Growth

An 8th grader wore sadness
like a wet coat, and slumped
inside it, he shone like a tear
on the face of 5th period.
"Hey kid," I said, "Want to teach
today?"
                His head jerked up,
blinked, blurted, "Ok...
then *you* go to McDonalds
for *your new job...*"
                                He met my eyes
and stood there, not moving,
then crashed into his seat.
He'd been for a moment upright
and abrupt, even brazen, but now,
face almost to his knees,
the kid would not look up. "Fine...
then *I'll* teach today," I said,
and we went each ahead, to be
as we had been before.

Saving Himself

Take the Cell Phone Parking Lot at Kennedy:
cabs, limos, me, Mr. Softee, and baseball
from many radios. Then a message "Here,"
and it's off to meet my wife. The "Here" of a life
might be the intersection of "waiting"
and "landed." Or what happens when
I call the roll, kids say, "Here,"
while what they mean is complex,
takes time to get a glimpse of.

Like Harlem Meer, a lake inside a city,
with turtles on. Men fishing, with purpose.
Thoreau said, "when a walk is failing
and you turn back, your numbness is a knocking,
at which Nature opens." Ducks rest
with one eye open in the sleep city allows.
Where Lenox heads north, a plane tree
of such height and width to have lived
across Harlem's several lives, stands,
spreading a green assertion. And here,

on 5th Ave a tour bus, luggage doors up,
a man sitting where suitcases go,
with his guitar and music. I heard rich notes.
I thought, no guitar case opened
for tips, no hat upturned, the bus driver
might be a man best right where he is,
mid-trip, saving himself.

Accord Reached

1.

I like to think of the Ravenswood El,
in Chicago, which ran beside the block
where my father was born, my grandfather
was long unemployed, and my parents
airless first apartment was so hot in summer
my father put her bed's feet in
their bathtub, which makes no sense
each time I think of it
unless he was afraid,
as a new husband, not to try.

2.

I like to think of a table and you
in that basement at the stove, for tea,
the boy friend and roommates out,
the hissing blue flame stove
beginning boil, your human
body leaning to adjust your
looking back from just
out of reach, as your smile
not about tea, loosened
my tourniquet,
my legs the first to know it
leapt, jerked, the table rocked,
the kettle sang, I could not stop
shaking, shaken, we looked
each other up, and grew solemn,
I like to think of being shaken
from fearing into chance.

Daily

She rises in the dark, coffee brewing
sighs brief music for her sleepy feet.
When she sits in pre-dawn to work,
the pulse of the house steadies; in an hour
she is off to shower but coffee mug is not
finished with her hands; when she dresses
for the day, her dissatisfaction is familiar
to listeners at home; her actual beauty
is about its own business, unaware;
when she leaves, the garage closes its one eye
and waits.
                    When she returns
she tells of a man long in hospital,
who was not to survive but sat, cheerful,
non-compliant, frail.
She could only listen in.
                                        Home, she finds
rice and chicken waiting, warming
as best they can; she finds wine in a clean
glass, then a second, is resting in her hand;
when she dresses for bed she wears
winter's flannel and if anyone is watching
his heart melts; she reads a single page
then sleeps, dreaming she's in an elevator
rising, on through the roof, up-going,
while on earth two dreamers sleep entangled.

Crossing the Delaware

"a crossing by water in winter to a shore
other than that the bridge reaches for"
—Frank O'Hara

I saw you napping in our riverside hotel,
exhaustion risen to meet chance, you
wearing your doctor's face, breathing steady.
We've landed in Pennsylvania for your birthday;

I stand on a headland, the very shore.
Awake, you say *Stop sighing...* Did I?... *Yes,*
you always do.... well, 40 years ago, we first
met the Delaware, now my breathing is

that exhale titled sigh, dizzy at how steep
there is beneath my feet. I don't look down;
we do go walking. A river refills itself.
A river goes between its banks not stopping once
to check. Houses here are faces we must have met;

now, wearing fresh paint, they watch us.
The canal, unused then, still empty, lovely,
having been well-built, bears small blue flowers
on its towpath, they look unafraid, to me,

but fear is not a word to use with flowers.
And that house sparrow? Seer without words
it might mark shapes getting in its way,
but not the long-married holding hands.

The Castlerigg Stone Circle, Cumbria,
– or Permanence

4,000 years ago humans set these stones
at bottom of a bowl of mountains, "It's obvious,"
Kevin says, "when you really look,
this was the center; of what is mystery."
How American of me to be giddy.
Grass never lost became this underfoot
that the latest sheep, not looking up
as we pass among them, chew.
It is not lonely here with stillness felt
as echo of an echo, this crowded air.

Home as a plain Bronx street,
stillness as the resting face of a house
earth bound by fists of cement,
stillness of water in a glass at bedside
over night, stillness of gasoline
at rest like little ponds
in the tanks of waiting cars,
stillness of a green garden hose
set forth by an older man
each year, carefully
circled on his driveway
in the exact place.

Ripeness Woven

As I walked up the hill to see the great
red oak, I thought of my grandfather, Pastor
Petrus Swarz, and I began to laugh: just
trust surprises. A man I never met,
Swedish immigrant who came with secrets
as a story, first pastor of Edgewater Baptist,
a man whose children, my aunts and uncles,
never spoke of him, who died 1939, is buried
somewhere, this man appears here?
A 300 year old oak is also not for us
to get to know. Unsatisfying to touch a tree.
To stand back is right.
Affection is not why I go to a forest,
though to be here is comforting.
It's possible to become empty
among trees, adding woody thoughts.
A tree in its forest seems to me stitched in,
while on a lawn a great tree gathers the air,
gathers presence from the open air
into a mass of presence and abides, erect.

The Lesson

Finding vocabulary for thought
in the valley of the Little Beaverkill,
early summer, meadow flowering, bird-full
ridge wrapped stillness of twilight.
We looked at each other and walked on.
The tents, the apparatus, fires, scent
of cooking in the common campground,
each family on its numbered and lettered space.
To walk among these, to hear thrushes'
silvered flutes from the almost dark,
to walk together bearing what our minds
with nothing to gain or prove, weave,
until looking at each other we see
the woven, wordless whole.

Surfaces

Crowded bus crossing the poorest borough.
No one is laughing in this "civic interior."
Many of the people are large, thick bodied.
It might be shift change at the nursing homes.
Patience in these faces might be the taut
wire walked between work and worry,
or between work and a small child.

Botanic Garden in the poorest borough.
After a chilly day, sun lights the tops of
trees soft brown. The forest thickens.
A family in the café – husband, wife, boy –
each with a purchase, plainly dressed,
are leaning in a little, each to each
at the small table. The boy thus protected,
is absorbed with his toy, the parents
watch each other and their child.

Later, at the bus stop, five people waiting,
I read from the face of my phone
about the coming bus, ".7 mile away."
A woman blurts, "The Garden is my default
when things, take my grandson, do not
go well." The Bx26 arrives. We sit apart.
On my visits I seek the Dawn Redwood:
The first description of it was based on
fossil needles from rocks millions of years old.
In 1941, a Chinese botanist travelling
through a remote section of central China,
discovered a population of living dawn redwoods.

Years later, living seeds sent across the world
enlarged it. Transferred to the Bx 10,

re-crossing the city, I like to imagine
that botanist. He must have been fully alive
to see what was not on the living list
alive, these that have stepped free
of the million years to stand silent
woody passengers of the turning earth.

III.

When This Is Working Well

When this is working well, 6 minutes apart,
10 cars, stained steel, fill and empty.
This is elemental. A mother
arrives and sits, her little girl kneels
to look out. Her little boy with – is it
a kaleidoscope? – sits next to the man
next to me. They talk. As mother watches

her boy mix in, her daughter with eyes on
the Bronx, riders look on, others look away,
the mother smiling seems to me a circle
in the air, of radiance, of protection for these
one does not want to leave us
in the steel car with plastic seats,
but nothing happens when they do

at 168 St., the hospital stop. The train
emptying to fill, a new mother seated,
a teenage daughter rests her head
on the shoulder of her parent. This, surely,
is the best that can befall a mother's trip,
she who might, on guard, also be at rest,
in this car, one of ten, 6 minutes from
the train behind it, if still well-spaced,
if all is working well. At 59th, a young man
shows a shining prosthetic leg but his body
is in spasm, and his begging-cup also shakes.
Giving $1, I bump the cup, its fall spills
bills coins and some man
already on his knees to help the kid

who's crying "sorry... please... so hungry,"
and now he *is* crying, naked among us,
he flees – at 28 Street – I walk too,
sign says train in 6 minutes then in 12 so
things are working well. Up on 7th Ave.
the sidewalk is roped off, kids are illustrating
Fashion Institute's wall w/cartoon shapes,
dream images weird and wooly, never seen
before right here and now, yet done
in colors straight from cans. It is a relief
to see this happen to cement.

Among Conifers

Think of 8th graders tripping and not falling,
not listening to whatever and yet
leafing out. They were
just kids sent to their room, it was
5th period, a schedule did it, and think
of standing among them: no one knows
what these will turn out to mean
who becoming turns inside out.

Think of the Botanical Garden, of standing
among Blue Atlas Cedars of Morocco rising
in the Bronx. Collectors did it: two are tall,
the third, smaller, has not yet spread itself.
A sign tells of life these facts: "the young tree
was planted as next generation to replace
the mature specimen behind it." To have read
this before; to read it again. Be not afraid.

It's a quick walk to the bridge. Upstream,
Bronx River descends by rapids, singing
about stone, then flows south, a surface
mirror smooth, a water-borne reflection
of leaves above in their pattern
of being alive. Now think of a man standing
on that bridge. He sees a mirror
but his face is not looking back at him

from leaves above the river on the river
he stands staring into
silenced and
cannot look away.

Rock and Tree

Tulip tree already gone sky high
to stand straight into its future tense.
I walked past it. Further in
a fallen tree lay quiet, softening,

beginning its long rebirth as earth.
Ahead, green hill became jagged rock face –
"Bear Den" – a sign for kids. When I walk
I think how rock is a thing

standing still, breathing stillness
into open time. I stopped beside
a tree of middle age, and spoke up.
"You were here before me and will be here

well after me." Ok, fine, but
it was too much with all this thinking!
I was on the uphill into forest,
a breeze had risen at my back

filling lifting rippling the leaves ahead alive,
each leaf doing things with air and light
I did not understand, I was just breathing
that which the rocks exhale.

A Room in the House of Time

In the city's forest, late autumn,
the path climbs gently to a hill's crown,
bare rock, striped with parallel lines
scraped across and often stepped on.
Just ahead is a sign. To read it
is to walk back, and repeat:
"glaciers advanced and retreated."

Here? "Four times..."

"The last time 14,000 years ago,"
but how grasp that as other than
printed words of earnest authority?

So, rocks under pressure past measuring
scraped this I stand on, rocks moving as
the ice moved? How believe that inched
retreat, a vastness none saw happen,
happened, here? How picture the depth

of ice on which no one ever stood,
chilled and imagining what was
how far below being scraped to bedrock
that became this, here, now?

As my questions empty
they settle at my feet, and silence
rises from bare rock
which has become a room
in the house of time,
a big old place,
ancient, open, and shut.

A Meditation

—"but is the earth as full as life was full, of them"
—Frank O'Hara

Why, when I'm writing with my
left hand, hold a book, one of the fathers,
in my right hand? Is it a counter weight
against tipping over? A long pole for balance
on the wire? Why is now an empty room,
no windows? Has my seeing run off with
someone new? The book I'm holding
is honest, flirty with the world, talky,
elusive, intense, unlikely as a father.

I do not know if what happened next
in the yard was a gift or an arrival
but I saw branches of a river birch burst
into brilliance. I cannot describe that.
I know a tree cannot assert itself.
I know something of what there is between us.
I know surprise separate from asking,
seeking that is not purpose, and
how much there is not to be afraid of,

like wisdom denying it is wise in that
book I held with taxis humming daytime
neon skirts above heels and jazz that births awe,
and of passion, "you don't refuse to breathe,
do you?" After that dies down he whispers,
From here, you find your own way home.

Other books by Kip Zegers
published by Dos Madres Press

The Poet of Schools (2013)
The Pond in Room 318 (2015)

He is also included in:
Realms of the Mothers:
The First Decade of Dos Madres Press - 2016

For the full Dos Madres Press catalog:
www.dosmadres.com